Puppy

Written by Rosalind Malam
Illustrated by Astrid Matijasevich

Sally's holiday had started badly. She'd let Henry, her budgie, out of his cage. That would be okay – if the windows were shut and the cat wasn't around. But this time she had left a window open. Henry had escaped!

Sally searched everywhere, but she never found Henry. She had a sinking feeling whenever she thought about him. Henry had gone – and it was her fault!

Henry! Where are you?

Mum asked if Sally would like to stay with Poppa for a bit. That helped to cheer her up. Poppa lived close to the sea.

It was wonderful staying with Poppa. They hunted for crabs in the rock pools. Poppa helped Sally make a kite. It soared like the seabirds – dipping and diving in the wind. They watched people fishing from the rocks. Sometimes they went fishing, too.

Every evening, Sally took Poppa's dog, Chip, for a walk.
They always followed the walkway that looked down
on the sea.

Before Sally knew it, it was the last day of her holiday. She took Chip out for their last walk.

The tide was still coming in. Sally watched the waves creep into the shore. She listened to the mud crabs. They made a cool noise – like popcorn in a pan.

The sun was low in the sky. Its light made a shimmering path across the water.

Sally called for Chip. It was time for them to go back. The seabirds were coming in to land.

Suddenly, Sally saw birds on the walkway. They were oystercatchers! Oystercatchers are shy and stay away from people. Something was wrong!

She soon saw what it was.

Two oystercatchers were tangled in a long fishing line. They were trying to get free!

The other oystercatchers wanted to help them. "P-peep! P-peep!" they called to their friends. But, the more the birds struggled, the more tangled they became.

Sally needed help to free the oystercatchers. It was getting dark. She didn't want to leave them.

"Help!" she yelled, over and over. But nobody was around.

245 – 65 million years ago

dinosaur

archaeopteryx
(ar-key-op-ter-ix)

65 million years ago – Today

eohippus
(ee-o-hip-us)

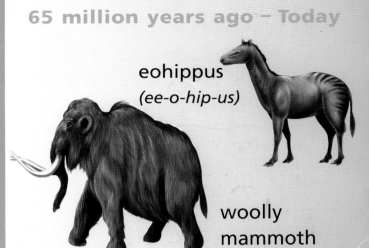

woolly
mammoth

snake   flower

frog

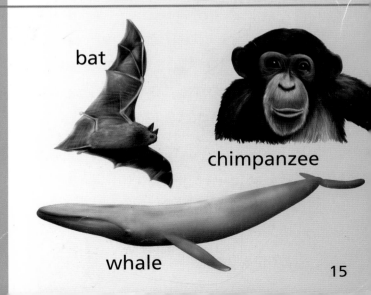

bat

chimpanzee

whale

15

Glossary

dinosaur an animal that lived on Earth many millions of years ago

fossils parts of animals and plants from long ago

fossil sites places where fossils are found

museums buildings where interesting things are kept, for everyone to see. Some of these things are very old.

palaeontologists scientists who dig up and study fossils

Index